T0086426

DIAMONDS
IN THE ROUGH

DONNA PUGLISI

authorHOUSE®

AuthorHouse™
1663 Liberty Drive
Bloomington, IN 47403
www.authorhouse.com
Phone: 1 (800) 839-8640

© 2017 Donna Puglisi. All rights reserved.

No part of this book may be reproduced, stored in a retrieval system, or transmitted by any means without the written permission of the author.

Published by AuthorHouse 03/03/2017

ISBN: 978-1-5246-7529-5 (sc)
ISBN: 978-1-5246-7528-8 (e)

Library of Congress Control Number: 2017903461

Print information available on the last page.

Any people depicted in stock imagery provided by Thinkstock are models, and such images are being used for illustrative purposes only. Certain stock imagery © Thinkstock.

This book is printed on acid-free paper.

Because of the dynamic nature of the Internet, any web addresses or links contained in this book may have changed since publication and may no longer be valid. The views expressed in this work are solely those of the author and do not necessarily reflect the views of the publisher, and the publisher hereby disclaims any responsibility for them.

Contents

Dedication

To all the "Diamonds In The Rough" in this world, I dedicate this book. Shine on and sparkle in your own unique way. Don't run with the crowd or feel the need to "blend".

Just be you!

It's not always the ones with the glam and glitter who try to outshine everyone else, but the silent, the subdued, the peaceful ones comfortable in their own skin who are the true

"DIAMONDS IN THE ROUGH"

Donna Puglisi

Diamonds In The Rough

Innocent, hopeful little faces,
These are the diamonds in the rough;
Will you weather life's challenges
when the going gets too tough?

You're the gems that don't glitter,
You're the gems that don't shine;
One day you'll be discovered
hidden in the mine.

Don't judge a book by its cover,
Who knows? They might be your next lover.
Look at the ones with all the tattoos,
Rings in the nose, no designer shoes;
Black polished nails and funny dyed hair,
People pass by and give them the stare.

That's when you dig a little deeper
for the ones with all the right stuff;
These are the sparkling jewels, my friend,
They're the diamonds in the rough.

The Scarred Face

As he descended from the street stairs, I saw his scarred, burned face. I was alone, walking along the river bank towards town.

No one was with me that day to hear me scream if he attacked me or pushed me in the river. I assumed the worst, just looking at this disfigured man.

He was a few strides behind me, as I quickened my pace. We walked in silence for what seemed to be an eternity. Around the bend, I felt him coming closer, and then I stopped.

I turned to face him and waited for him to catch up with me. Somehow I wasn't afraid anymore. He gave me the biggest smile! I smiled back and we continued to walk together. He was a middle-aged Mexican who had the kindest brown eyes I've ever seen. They sparkled beneath his ravaged leathery skin.

As we walked and talked, he told me about the tragedy years ago. He lost his family and friends in a paint factory fire. He was the only one who survived, but his emotional scars cut deeper than any on his face. He was forever reminded of that fateful day every time he looked in the mirror.

Somehow I saw only beauty in him as I listened to him talking about his family and his life. This stranger, who I feared in the beginning because of his disfigurement, suddenly became a beautiful person. He taught me never to judge anyone before I had a chance to know them.

I discovered my diamond in the rough that day.

Big Wheelers
(The Real Diamonds)

Rolling thunder on two big wheels,
Iron legs replacing withered limbs.
They're a force to be reckoned with,
No fear, as they race down narrow hallways.

NASCAR for seniors!

Who were they in younger days?
These Big Wheelers had their day in the sun,
Some now only shadows creeping along walls,
Some just shells of what they used to be.

But the mighty Big Wheelers still roll on,
Undeterred by Time,
that eternal thief, stealing their youth and bodies.

Stoic, proud, determined not to wither and die,
They're the old diamonds,
the ancient gems hidden in the ground
still shining, waiting to be unearthed and appreciated
for their inner beauty and timeless wisdom.

Respect the Big Wheelers, for each one has a story to tell
to those who are

willing
to
listen

———⌇⌇∽∾⌒⊙⌒∾∽⌇⌇———

No Time Like The Present

Now is the time to say those words
you've always meant to speak to those you love,
those precious gems who mean so much.

Don't take for granted a brand new day,
a new start, a new way to say

"I love you"

Because each day
is a gift from God

Fractured

(THE DISINTEGRATION OF A FAMILY)

There once was a family who had it all,
Or so it seemed to be;
There once was a family whose world had no limits,
Envied by all to see.

But egos and lust seeped through the cracks
in their palace made of lies;
Shameless affairs, deceit, haughty airs,
No one heard their midnight cries.

Ripped at the seams, their lofty dreams
fell apart one by one;
Darkness descended, then the rain,
Black clouds obscured the sun.

Hazy nights marred by drugs,
Victims of thieves and thugs;
The thorns grew thick around their wall,
A fortress made of glass.

Oh, how the mighty eventually fall,
Invincible on their thrones;
The final crack in the thin veneer,
Now zombies, they walk like drones.

There once was a family who had it all,
Or so it seemed to be.

—————ᘛ⁀ᗢ⁀ᘚ—————

I Saw A Blind Man

I saw a blind man, but he didn't see me,
I looked at him feeling the day;
I wished he could see the beauty before him,
But he did, in his own special way.

With my eyes wide open, he saw more than me,
Felt the rush of warm wind in his hair;
Every sound, every smell, one with the world, I could tell,
Sensing my curious stare.

My jealous orbs strained to see
his invisible canvas hidden from me;
Feeling the colors, warm and cool,
a soft breeze kissed my cheek.
I closed my eyes, as his from birth,
As one, we did not speak.

The tapping of his cane swept the ground,
Defining his space from those around;
He turned to me, and with a smile,

He told me
I was
Beautiful

Face Book

Every face tells a story,
I know yours well;
Life's map and journeys are etched in your Face Book.

Rings on a tree reveal its age,
I've studied your face, every line, every page;
Each wrinkle and laugh line,
A crease here and there,
Your furrowed brow tells me how much you care.

Don't change a thing, stay as you are,
Your Face Book is honest, every defect and scar;
Your life in deep layers, each thought and each deed,
Wounds opened wide,
Cuts left to bleed.

Unique is your physique,
Uncompromising your look;
No, don't change a thing,
I love your Face Book!

The Boneyard

The pastures were green and lush,
Rivers ran wild and free;
Everyone was happy,
Everyone but me.

I often wondered what's out there,
Was there something better than this?
Better people, better life,
What in the world did I miss?

Finally after much travel,
I stumbled to the end,
It was a dusty boneyard,
No one there to befriend.

All alone I wandered,
Searching for my pastures green,
But all I found were bleaching bones,
Flesh no more, picked clean.

The boneyard was my misfortune,
I didn't know what I had;
Searching for what I left behind,
My judgement had been bad.

Alone and scared I came home to my oasis in the sand,
Gazed upon my perfect world,
Sparkling jewels in my hand.

Sometimes it takes a boneyard to make you realize
You don't have to wander far,
It's right before your eyes!

First Impression

He was a decorated hero in Navy blue,
A brave young pilot in World War II;
His dentures clicked every time he talked,
Shuffling slowly, a limp when he walked.

He wore a toupe, askew on his head,
Slight wisps of hair, white tinged with red;
His kind, wrinkled face showed years in the sun,
Eyes of light blue twinkled mischief and fun.

"Welcome to WalMart!", he said with a grin,

Don't judge a man till you know where he's been!

The Grounds Keeper

He raised his rake as if it were Don Quixote's sword,
cutting a swath through the jungle of weeds;
He was a true pirate, captain of his own ship,
steadfast and swarthy.
His face was tanned and creased, with twinkling eyes straining as
he moved mountains of dirt with his mighty shovel.

The Grounds Keeper was king of his domain,
oblivious to the relentless sun
beating down upon his furrowed brow.

Intent on his conquest of the lush foe before him,
he worked through the night;
Only the moon and stars were his companions.

Intent and dedicated to his profession,
he had the strength of a Titan.
The Grounds Keeper, bent with age,
surveyed the land before him;
A worthy opponent, he was awed by its beauty.

He was the diamond buried in the very earth
he lovingly cared for.

Tattoo

You got under my skin like a flaming tattoo,
You're the dye running through my veins;
Bright reds, your laughter,
Deep blue, your tears,
Every pore bleeds with your loving stains.

Colors fade, not memories,
You're my favorite pair of jeans;
Sharing secrets, you're the heart of me,
Timeless,
Eternal,
I wear you for all to see.

———⁓⁓⊶⊶⊙⊶⊙⊶⊙⊶⊙⊶⊙⊶⊙⊶⊙⊶⊙⊶⊙⊶———

In Between

I want to see beyond stark reality,
The realm beyond black and white.

Shades of gray between
night and day,
The depths of perceptions
are the true connections,

Shaded in the paleness of gray.

The Waitress

She blended in with the wallpaper, nothing special.
She was just doing her job in her greasy apron,
Taking orders from the boss,
Taking orders from everyone.
A few coins they toss, looking past her face,
Not really seeing her because
she was just a waitress.

Unassuming she plodded on, weary eyes, long hours
for meager pay.
"Some day I'll be rich", she said,
"Some day before they find me dead in bed".

For years she scraped by, saving every dime,
Never complaining, biding her time;
One day she left, never looked back,
Drove off in her shiny new Cadillac.
She lived in a house on top of a hill,
Pool in the back with a waterfall's spill.

No one remembered who she was,
After all, she was just a waitress.

———

Fragile

How fragile we are!
We break like fine china when we hit the wall,
Breaking bones with every fall;
Sometimes we forget our place,
In the scheme of things,
We fall from Grace.

Against nature's force we will surely lose,
Battered, bleeding with every bruise;
Spirits unbroken, undaunted we fight,
The deluge, non-stop,
No blue skies in sight.

The Human Race will continue to war,
Destroying ourselves forever more;
Religion and politics set the world adrift
in a sea of madness, nothing left.

Swimming against the tide,
Mouths open wide,
Swallowed whole, fighting for air,
Praying for help, no one to care.

God, help your children when we lose our way,
Words leave us mute, nothing to say;
Bless us with your enduring Love,
For we are truly

Fragile

One Little Letter

One little thought, one little letter,
Changed someone's life all for the better;
The power of the pen, a good thought to share,
One good deed shows how much you care.

He was a little old man stooped with age,
shuffling his feet on the floor;
His welcoming smile lit up the room,
The first one you saw at the door.

"Welcome to the movies, my friends,
What are you seeing today?"
He ripped up the tickets and with a smile said,
"Enjoy, and have a good day!"

Through rain or shine, good days and bad,
That little old man gave it all he had;
One day I wrote a very kind letter
praising this kind old man;
I let the boss know we loved him so,
and I was his number one fan!

Moving slowly to the door,
He smiled and then he asked once more,
"May I take your tickets? Enjoy the show",
beaming with an inner glow.

He hugged me with thanks with his old withered arms,
Then, much to my surprise,
He said, "You made me feel like a king!"
as tears welled up in his eyes.

One little thought, one little letter,
Changed someone's life all for the better.

Swinging On A Tire

Higher and higher the old tire swings,
Through the trees I can touch the marshmallow clouds;
Skimming rainbows, I have wings like a bird,
Reaching the stars, kissing the sun,
Dodging raindrops without a care in the world.

Those wonderful, carefree days!

I wrap myself in a fantasy world
as the old tree groans to hold me,
Twisted limbs reach out to play,
I'm swinging on a tire!

I am the Queen, I am the royal eagle,
I am the free spirited fairy;
There are no boundaries, no walls to hold me
as I fly higher and higher toward Heaven.

Angels sit on my tiny shoulders,
Their mischievous laughter echoes
through the babbling brooks and whispering winds,

Ah, those wonderful carefree days!

Hope

Out of the barrenness, out of the depths of nothingness,
She blossoms.

Through the jagged rock and ice,
she struggles to break free;
Her delicate flowers sparkle like tiny diamonds.

Though the odds are against her,
She thrives, a lone survivor
in a cold cruel world.

I call her HOPE.

HOPE rises from the ashes
to become a beautiful flower.
From the dark abyss and gloom,

She is the Light,

She is
HOPE

———————

Fields Of Lavender

The lush fields of purple perfume
were so surreal, so inviting.

It was Heaven on earth,
One body of motion, swaying in the gentle summer wind,
Jasmine breezes mingled with
the passion in his violet eyes.

That was a summer to remember,
The summer of love and laughter,
lilacs and fields of lavender.

In his arms I danced wild and free,
Childish giggles when he looked at me;
As I melted in his gaze,
I knew he was mine, always, always.

Alone in our universe, warm erotic days,
A world of two in love;
We were happy
in our fields of lavender.

So Lazy

He was so lazy, he was smart,
He made it look like a work of art!
Dodging this, dodging that,
He's a pain in the ass, a devious cat.

Pointing fingers, "It's not my fault,
Not in my job description!"
He's the guy you love to hate,
The alien in science fiction.

Pass the buck, side-step the muck,
Let everyone drown in quick sand;
He rose through the ranks,
Not a word of thanks,
Your loyalty he will demand.

The lazy cat is getting fat,
Indulging in spoils of war;
One of these days he'll pay his dues,
as his butt is kicked out the door.

The higher you go, the farther you fall,
It's a long way down as you plummet;
The corporate ladder has many steps,
A treacherous climb to the summit.

Beware of that slippery slope, dear friends,
Envy, back-stabbing never ends;
What's the thing we all desire?
Getting out of the rat race and
RETIRE!

———⟶◦⟋◦⟍◦◦⟋◦◦∿∿———

Cocoon

She was wrapped in herself, oblivious to all,
Tightly protected within her self-made cocoon;
Silk threads smothered past sins and lovers
left to smolder in ashes.

Tangled webs of deceit and lies, woven with precision;
When will she emerge from her decaying tomb of silence,
only to spread her wings again, satiating her ravenous appetite?

Like a locust, she devoured innocents, savoring every bite,
Destroying everything before her,
Naked and full of empty victories she succumbed
to the rotting grave awaiting another cycle
in her poisonous rampage.

No butterfly emerges, only a prickly thorn,
Cursed from the very day she was born;
She is a creature to abhor,
Seductress, hungering to rise once more.

—ᴡᴏᴏᴄᴇᴛᴏᴏᴛᴇᴏᴏᴡ—

Patchwork Quilt

He stitched a quilt with years of guilt,
Watching his blanket grow;
Sewn together day by day,
His secrets did not show.

With every sin and dirty deed,
His precious patches began to bleed;
Like Dorian Gray's portrait,
His face was pure,
He thought he fooled the world, for sure.

An invisible cloak, wrapped up in lies,
His laughter and youth were his disguise;
Through the years, he fell apart,
His quilt no longer a work of art;
Edges frayed, like jangled nerves,
A fitting end a sinner deserves.

Dining On A Slab

Concrete tables, bricks for mats,
Coins and dollars tossed in their hats;
Waving to people crossing the street,
"Feed me, please! I've nothing to eat!"

Outdoor dining, no reservations,
Catching wisps of conversations;
Dining on a slab, hiding in doorways,
No one looks at them eye to eye;
Invisible, blending in with the cold hard concrete,
No one cares to hear them cry.

Lost in a turbulent sea of humanity,
Drowning as we sip champagne;
Haunting dull eyes searching for the light,
We turn a blind eye to their suffering and pain.

Dining on a slab tonight,
The moon is full, the stars are bright;
Clink, clink! The coins are thrown without care,
Don't look too hard with your haughty stare.

Laughter echoes across the street,
Oblivious to those who have nothing to eat.
Those forgotten souls of misfortune,
Ragged rejects of mankind;
Shadows of men, hiding in doorways,
With eyes wide open, we are truly blind.

———————

Wonder

A baby's first breath,
Pure innocence and love,
That is the beauty of wonder!

Let me gaze upon the world with angelic eyes,
Greet each day as a sweet surprise;
God bless me with serenity,
Cast away darkness so I can see.

Never let me become so jaded,
To view my life as beauty faded;
Always be a child at heart,
embracing life with a fresh new start.

Don't listen to the drone of hum drum,
Don't let it pull you under;
The rose is best without her thorns,
Let me bask in the Splendor of Wonder!

Jewel Thief

You stole my most precious jewel,
my shining gem;
In the gloomy night you tiptoed in,
smothering the light from her soul.

Jewel thief, stealthy, velvet black your cloak,
You stole my life from me.

Is death so final, closing the door forever?
I know I'll see her on the other side,
So I just go along with the tide,
knowing I'll find my precious jewel
once again.

Grandma Was A Tomboy

Small and spunky, hair cut short,
Outplaying boys in every sport;
Flying freckles, running bases,
Crossing her eyes, making funny faces.

"It's not a crime to be four feet tall,
You'll see, I'll be the best of all!"
Climbing trees, scraping knees,
Catching frogs, rolling logs.

Wear a dress? What a mess!
It was like giving a cat a bath;
Screaming, kicking, what a licking,
That was Grandma's wrath.

She was Wendy and her Lost Boys,
Surrendering her youth to age;
Fell in love, a bride, a mom,
Turning life's endless page.
She never lost her "Peter Pan",
Eyes twinkling with joy;
Mischievous, sassy, always classy,
Grandma's still a Tom Boy!

Boomerang

"What goes around comes around",
The circle is infinite and true;
Don't try to run, don't try to hide,
Boomerang Karma sticks like glue.

We dig our own graves, a lifetime deep,
Tossing and turning with guilt as we sleep;
Like the Reaper, Boomerang waits at your door,
knocks you unconscious as you hit the floor.

You knew this day would come, my friend,
Pay your dues, this is your end;
Boomerang Karma, those taunting twins,
await the day we account for our sins.

Each name is recorded, etched in tombstone,
Boomerang Karma won't leave you alone!

Ill-Wind

An ill-wind blew across the land,
destroying the Home of The Free;
An ill-wind toppled mighty oaks,
exposed for all to see.

This ill-wind cast an ominous cloud,
Angry voices rang out loud;
Distrust and dissent divided a nation,
It was the beginning of disintegration.

The ill-wind blew across the seas
as the devil danced on foreign soil;
Dogs of war let loose the fires
amidst hatred and turmoil.

The lands lay barren, scorched and black,
By now, there was no turning back;
Destruction caused by evil men,
We've seen this time and time again.

Let calm winds prevail and shift the tides of war,
Let peace be king as eagles soar;
May God smile on our Promised Land
and make our people understand.

A perfect world is fantasy,
We dream of peace and harmony;
But dreams are what made this nation great,
Daring men don't hesitate.
Stand up tall for all to see we truly are
THE LAND OF THE FREE!

I Saw It In Your Eyes

They say the eyes are the windows to the soul,
I looked deep into yours,
Light and loving, good and kind,
The one everybody adores.

You catch me when I fall,
If you didn't care, you wouldn't be there at all;
Swinging in rhythm as two on a trapeze,
I reach for you knowing you'll grab me with ease.

No net is needed, your arms are strong,
Safe and secure, with you I belong.

Love is true,
It never lies;
You belong to me,

I saw it in your eyes

Four Walls

She finally escaped her four walls
that became her personal prison;
At last she's free!

Free to fly anywhere she desires, on the wings of a bird,
Floating peacefully down a lazy stream;
Free at last, not bound by structure,
Not bound to earth's ties.

She's my angel,
She has eternity at her fingertips;
She is one with the universe now.

Toxic

Poison ivy, red flags, warning flashing lights,
Ignoring the signs in front of me,
I drank from your toxic brew;
Nothing could satisfy my ravenous appetite,
Craving toxic you.

When do we ever learn to run before disaster strikes?
The eye of the hurricane, the "perfect storm",
Tsunami's rushing waters,
I'm drowning.

I didn't know you were toxic.

———ⵡⵙⴰⵎⴰ———

Daddy's Little Girl

He was wrapped around her fingers
the moment she was born;
She was daddy's little girl,
a rose without a thorn.

As time went by the thorns grew thick
with every word and deed;
No one dared approach her,
for fear she'd make them bleed.

The rose turned black, the thorns grew dense,
enveloping her heart;
Open to ridicule and scorn,
Her whole world fell apart.

Daddy's little girl was daddy's cross to bear,
She sat alone in her cold, dark room
with a blank and distant stare.

The prickly rose became a weed,
unsightly, disenchanted;
For days on end, he heard her screams,
wild, untamed, she ranted.

Undaunted, daddy cradled her when hope began to fade,
Wiping tears from her eyes, he listened, unafraid.
With love and patience, his little rose began to see the light,
The thorns fell off and petals bloomed,
She won her bloody fight.
She's daddy's little girl again, sunshine frames her face,
Pure love won out and saved her when she
took her fall from Grace.

———⁓⁓⊙⊙⊙⊙⁓⁓———

Falling Through The Cracks

Falling through the cracks are the lost ones,
Drowning in the muck and the mire;
Tossed aside, left to die,
Burned in the funeral pyre.

Falling like dust from the rafters
through the cracks of an old rotting barn;
No "happy ever-afters", no one to protect them from harm.

These are the lost ones in limbo,
There is no Heaven or Hell;
Talking to no one, talking out loud,
Yes, you know them well.

These are the ones you pass on the street,
Don't stare too long, be discreet.
Faceless, nameless, they wither and fall,
Too many to count, just bury them all.

Trying to keep pace with the human race,
Trampled on when they stumble;
God help your children, the small and the weak,
Bring the arrogant to their knees, make them humble.

Falling through the cracks,
Catch them if you can;
Their faces are ours,
They are Every Man.

———woooooooo———

When Beauty Is The Beast

What lies beneath that beautiful face,
behind the paint and glitter?
What happened to your inner soul
to make your heart so bitter?

You hide the hideous beast within,
smiling through a life of sin.
Adoring fans can't see a flaw,
Unaware, they stare in awe.

What would they say if you melt away,
exposing decay inside?
You wear it well, no one can see
your mask of pretentious pride.

When beauty is the beast she thrives in her deception,
Hypnotic like a Siren's trance,
Disguised in false perception.

Predator, she'll wear you down,
False queen she wears a thorny crown;
Beauty ages, wearing thin,
Only then will you see the beast within.

———∽∾∾⌇⌇∾∽———

Mermaids

Sweet nymphs of the sea,
Daughters of Poseidon,
Shimmering skin of scales;
Dancers of the deep blue ocean,
Skimming waves with emerald tails.

A sailor's dream, a sailor's curse,
With every song, with every verse;
Along the shores on jagged rocks,
Enticing ships at sea;
Lonely men so far from home,
Now a distant memory.

Sing, Enchantress, through gills and fins,
Make every soul forget his sins;
Swim with the fish, half woman be,
A mermaid's flesh you'll never see.

She's cursed from birth between two worlds,
Never a mortal's wife;
That is her fate for eternity,
That is the mermaid's life.

Jambalaya

We live in a world of Jambalaya,
A constant stew, a mixed-up brew;
Stir the pot, don't let it rot,
That wonderful hot Jambalaya!

Diverse as a spicy concoction of ghost pepper chili,
the Jamba Samba dances willy nilly;
This old globe keeps turning, churning,
Defying gravity, rocket boosters burning.

Stars and planets, those timeless spinning orbs
since the dawn of time,
Dance in this big universal pot,
Eternal entities all part of that wicked,
delicious jumble of juicy Jambalaya!

A Dove's Song

The stillness and calm of the morning,
A fresh new beginning.

Silence is only broken by the soft cooing of a dove,
So gentle and caressing, she kisses my cheek
with her velvet song.

She calms my soul in the early hours,
For we are silent observers
of a new day not yet disturbed.

———ᴍᴏᴏᴄᴛᴏᴏᴛᴏᴏᴍ———

Blood Red

Cutting across the sky like a knife on flesh,
The blood red sunsets bleed;
Hues of orange and yellow blend with
the night before brooding darkness descends.

No painter can duplicate what God has intended,
Each sunset His unique creation;
Absorb its beauty as the sky's aglow,
Nature's putting on one hell of a show!

Night shrouds blood red in black,
Once a sunset's gone,
You can't get her back.

Dawn

Pink ribbons sweep across the sky,
slowly changing to gold;
A soft canvas of clouds sets the new morning's cinema.

This is a show of delicate balance and order.
Before the noise of a busy day breaks the seductive silence,
there is only awe
as I watch the changing colors of dawn.

Clouds

Lying on our backs on the grass,
Gazing up at the clouds;
Beautiful creatures, changing into animals,
In a second, just ghostly wisps of nothingness!

Marshmallows, mashed potatoes
decorate the sky,
Reaching up to touch them,
Wishing we could fly!

Haunting figures stretch their frail bony fingers,
Twisting, turning on a whim,
Don't blink! They're gone...

Moving fast, the teasing clouds
Constantly paint their new canvas,
Limited only to our imaginations!

Floating On Diamonds

Slivers of silver in the sun,
Shimmering specs on the water;
Gently rocking sleepy boats,
Drifting in and out of a dream
On a lazy summer day.

I'm in a trance, my soul is at peace,
I'm floating on diamonds!

One with the world, I'm a jewel,

Shining on a sea of jade.

Winged Angels Of The Sea

Flying angels gliding through liquid air, the deep purples and blues
of the ocean;
The Manta Rays swim freely,
peaceful in their dark world beneath.

Velvet winged creatures stroke the waves,
Graceful, mysterious dancers of the sea;
Gentle giants riding the bubbles of divers
in awe of these ancient beauties before them.

Mantas! Cloaked kings, ruling, benevolent spirits,

God's gift to His kingdom below.

———⌇∿⊙⟲⊙⟲⊙∿⌇———

Sublime

Under the canvas of stars and the blanket of
the sensuous night,
white birch trees surrounded us,
silent observers of frozen kisses
wet with promises and desire,
lingering frosty ghosts in the cold crisp air.

Sublime!

Serene and sexy, the lake beckoned us,
blue-black her face,
reflecting twinkles of starlight,
envious, enticing,
waiting to caress our naked bodies
should we chance to invade her frigid waters.

Careless and free, tossing inhibitions aside,
we danced like natives among the private
audience of those white sentinels.
Stoic and solid, rigid protectors with
limbs extended, uninvited dance partners
as we became one with the night, invisible to the world.

Sublime!

—⁓⁓⊙⊙⊙⊙⊙⊙⁓⁓—

Riding The Thermals

How free!

Precision.

Nature's gliders hovering, suspended in time,
Riding the thermals!

Floating on clouds of silk,
They are whispers in the wind.

Swoosh! Swoosh!

Envious am I, wishing I was flying on a tailwind,
But my clumsy arms, flapping frantically
in my fantasy flight can't compare to
your natural grace.

———ᘉᘉᗥᗣᘉᗣᗣᗥᗣᘉᘉ———

The Grand Dames

Towering ladies with withered arms stretch toward the sky,
wearing their tattered remnants of summer and fall.

Long, outstretched fingers dangle feathered moss, like boas
around their old veined necks.

These are the old ones – the regal ladies,
The Grand Dames, revered trees of the South.

Bending to reach each other in windy conversations,
they embrace across the dusty roads.

Aching in weariness of ages, but still dressed in mossy glory,
They wear their feathered hats of leaves;
Proudly they stand for show,
Proudly they speak to those who will look and listen
to their stories of years past.

These are the beautiful Grand Dames of the South.

———ᴡᴏᴏᴇᴦᴅᴏᴋᴏᴏᴡ———

Being Betty White

When I get old I want to be
just like Betty White!
Not worried about anything I say,
whether it's wrong or right.

A twinkle in my eye, an impish grin,
An off-color joke, is that a sin?
A dimpled cheek, a sassy smile,
Baggy sweats I'll wear in style.

My girlish charm will take me far,
If my keys are taken, won't drive a car;
With a laugh and a giggle,
My old bod will jiggle,
Incontinence abounds;
Is this how it ends, wearing "Depends"?
Will my butt make funny sounds?

Yes, being Betty White is out of sight,
I couldn't have chosen better;
I'll be so discreet on my designer rubber sheet,
This old gal won't be a bed-wetter!

I'm sure Betty White won't really mind
if I steal her spark or thunder;
By the time I'm her age,
She'll be off the stage
and buried six feet under!

The Natural Order

In nature, there is a natural order to things,
The sun's warm rays and life it brings;
A time to awaken, a time to sleep,
A time for prayers and hopes we keep.

Birds build nests for eggs to hatch,
From twigs and straw,
they weave and thatch;
No one tells them what to do,
It's nature's way of loving you.

Lush green forests bring life to all,
From giant trees to creatures small;
Wildlife with no boundaries,
Nature's children roaming free!

God's creations on this earth,
Seasonal changes bring rebirth;
Keep our earth alive and clean,
Her oceans blue and forests green.

We're all a part of nature's plan,
to live together, beast and man;
Let's not forget the role we play,
Love each other, as is God's way!

Knock-Kneed In Knickers

"Knock, knock, who's there?"
They'd all make fun of me and stare;
To cover up my bony knees and
stop their taunting snickers,
I bought myself a brand new pair of
brown tweed baggy knickers!

Knickers are a kind of "bloomers"
kids wore long ago,
I guess they were the rage back then
so your bony knees don't show.

I only wore them just to hide my knees
touching each other;
No one knew how to straighten them,
Not even my dear sweet mother.

Such is life, thank God for knickers,
They saved my life in school;
As you know, it's really tough
when kids can be so cruel.

Knock-kneed in knickers way back then,
Now I wear long pants;
I'm popular with the girls, they say,
and have a fighting chance!

You won't catch me in a pair of shorts,
Oh no, that's not for me!
I'm happy in a pair of jeans and walking knee-to-knee!

Invasion Of The Love Bugs!

Red and black flying fornicators
blacken the skies twice a year;
Annoying, spermy globs on windshields,
Don't wipe them off, they smear!

Crawling, covering cars until you can't open a door,
Swarming in, they wiggle, attached,
Mating on the floor!

Just get a room! Disgusting display of intercourse as they fly,
God's creatures, yes, but what was He thinking?
To punish us? But why?!

Love bugs, love bugs,
Don't bug us anymore;
I'd like to squish you as you hit my door!

Thank God you're slow as you fly together,
Swatting you is easy;
The problem's appalling, my car needs overhauling,
Why the hell are you so greasy?

———∿∽⊙⋆⊙⊱∽∿———

Peachy, Pinky Cheeks Of Cheery!

Oh, don't you love to pinch those pudgy baby cheeks?
No words to say, just wants to play,
Don't squeeze too hard, it leaks!
Those pink balloons protruding from that chubby little face,
Drooling, gurgling, spitting food,
Splattering all over the place!

Little peachy pinky cheeks of cheery,
Make you laugh when you feel weary;
Pooping, eating, always feeding,
We love when they indulge;
Roly poly baby fat,
Baggy diapers bulge!

Enjoy them now while you can,
before they start to talk;
Pop your vitamins, take your pills,
Those cheeks are gonna walk!
Here and there, everywhere,
Your eyes are bloodshot and bleary;
Beware of that cute little toddler
with those pinky cheeks of cheery!

Joint Session

Snap! Crackle! Pop! Crack!

My whole body is out of whack!
From the top of my spine
To the tip of my toes,
My joints are popping,
That's just how it goes!

Every move's an effort
as I try to climb the stairs;
There's no garage to change my tires,
I've got too many repairs!

Just give that oil can a shake or two,
Lubricate my knees;
Elbows, wrists, shoulders, neck,
Every pinky, please!

This joint session has run its course,
I have no regrets, no remorse;
With bills piled high, I heave a sigh,
Praying to God, I ask Him why?
Dear Father, when your plan was made
to create the human body,
Why didn't you plan to make a "Bionic Man"
who never grows old or shoddy?

Sipping Single

Surrounded by testosterone,
A single lady, all alone;
Quick side glances, hoping for more romances,
A wink, a blink,
Subtle flirtations,
Dirty martinis,
Dirty sensations.

What's a gal to do?

Any way you look at it,
You're on the rocks!
It's sink or swim, hanging on an occasional whim,
Sipping single, try to mingle,
Stand out in a crowd by laughing out loud;
Amidst the chaos of crunching bodies,
I still find myself

Sipping single

Shelf Life

Muttering to myself, no one listens,
No audience to hear what I say;
I feel like a spec of dust on a shelf,
Why the hell am I talking anyway?

A woman's not to be ignored,
Conversation falls on deaf ears;
His back is turned, he's bored to death,
A painful rut, married too many years.

I'd like a total facelift, my body's living proof,
My shelf life has expired and menopause has hit the roof!
Hubby has the dreadful plan that soon he'll be retiring,
Annoying me all day and night,
My God! Why am I perspiring?

Splotches of red dot my once pretty face,
I know I'm definitely not blushing;
Incontinence abounds as I make the rounds
and the toilet's always flushing!

Yes, I'm way beyond repair,
Same old bras and underwear;
What can I lose? Should I hit the booze?
Maybe I should wear a thong;
What else can possibly go wrong?

Oh, yes...
Till death do us part!

No Socks Today!

"The little black bear climbed up a tree..."
"The little black bear climbed up a tree..."
"The little black bear climbed up a tree..."

It didn't make any sense to me!

Over and over and over again I grasped the chalk that was my pen;
In the corner I faced the wall,
punished and ridiculed by all.

As the others went out to play,
I sat alone because
I wore no socks today!

My feet exposed, toes seen by all,
Giggles and fingers pointed as my tears began to fall;
Gathered 'round the teacher, we sat on the floor,
As she played piano, I wanted to bolt for the door.

One little boy took pity on me,
He covered my toes so no one would see;
I'll never forget that kind little gesture,
My tears faded away;
Second grade's not fun when
you wear no socks today!

Looking For Road Kill
At Maggie's Diner

"YOU KILL 'EM, WE GRILL 'EM!"

Vultures sitting on telephone lines,
Waiting for the next road kill;
Brunch or dinner, it's a winner
If it's dead, get your fill!

C'mon down to Maggie's Diner
for the best road kill in town;
Get it while it's fresh and warm,
It's better than ground round!

Well done or rare? With that dead eye stare,
the vultures quench their thirst;
The tricky thing is nab that thing,
So you can get there first.

Don't like the menu? Don't look too hard,
Don't read the warning sign;
'possum meat is really sweet,
And raccoon tastes just fine.

Yes, folks just rave about Maggie's Place,
Eating road kill is no disgrace;
Just don't ask questions, chew your meal,
Mmm! We love that rubbery feel.

Who needs a four-star restaurant
When you can dine right here?
The food is fresh, right off the hoof,
What's your preference, dear?

Cherry Pie

Ah, that wonderful aroma of mom's freshly baked cherry pie
wafting through the air, tantalizing and teasing,
sitting all alone on the kitchen window sill!

I remember those days as a boy
playing ball on a hot summer day;
Running through the sheets hung out to dry,
Hurrying to get a taste of mom's cherry pie!

The smell would fill the house and yard,
As I shook off the day's clinging dust;
I couldn't wait to taste that wonderful concoction
Of cherries and crispy brown crust.

I can still see her pie sitting on the window sill,
So pretty and brown and warm;
It took all my strength to ignore that sweet pie,
Until later like locusts we'd swarm.

Mom always knew I loved cherry pie,
She'd bake them one after another;
With love and a pinch of laughter thrown in,
Oh, how I loved my mother!

Apple is nice, pumpkin is good,
Blueberry places a close second;
But my cherry pie wins the blue ribbon for sure,
"Come eat me!" the red cherries beckoned.

I think cherry pie is like a best friend,
Comforting, always at ease;
Don't clear the table, cherry pie's for dessert!
Can you cut me another slice please?

Tag Along

She was annoying, she was small,
She was a baby, the youngest of all;
Tag along, my shadowy friend,
"Blood sisters", loyal to the end.

True blue, we stick like glue,
Bubble gum buddy, my silly putty;
Dragging your little red wagon,
Raggedy Ann and Andy,
Turkish taffy, cotton candy.

Barbie dolls and slinky,
Swear to be true, pull my pinky;
Love you more, I swear,
Give you a wedgie, yank your underwear!

Stick out your tongue, cross your eyes,
Your nose will grow with all those lies!
Nag along, tag along, baby doll,
Scrape a knee, pick you up when you fall.

My Tinker Bell, my Peter Pan,
I love you, kid, I'm your biggest fan!
Flying by my side, you do belong,
You're my shadowy friend,

My tag along!

Gossip

Clickety, clackity, yack, yack, yack,
Once you've said it, you can't take it back;
One false rumor is like a tumor,
Growing fast as cancer;
Lightning, ZAP! It's a gossiper's trap,
There is no time to answer.

"She said this, and he said that,
What a juicy story! What a terrible spat!"
The story grows like a liar's nose,
Phone lines are lit and burning;
A witch's brew, a poisonous stew,
Tidal waves of gossip churning.

Little clicks of wagging tongues,
Green monsters in disguise;
Self-righteous in their cloistered world,
Don't listen! A word to the wise.

Clickety, clackity, yack, yack, yack,
Once you've said it,

You can't take it back!

Crepe Paper

(On aging skin)

Covering my body from head to toe,
My skin used to have a youthful glow;
Now it's withered and starting to flake,
I look like crepe paper, for goodness sake!

Wrinkles here and wrinkles there,
Wrinkles in my underwear;
No miracle cream or youthful gel
can help me from not aging well.

Botox worked a year ago,
But how to stop the carnage below?
Knees are knobby twisted things,
My arms look like two chicken wings!
My belly button dropped an inch,
No collagen left where I dare to pinch.

I think I'll drape myself in crepe,
That will be my great escape;
I'll blend in with that old wallpaper
shredded with a painter's scraper.

Snakes shed their skin and start anew,
Why can't I just do that too?
I'd love skin smooth as a baby's butt,
Muscled, toned and really cut!

I'm resigned to sag and crinkle,
Why can't I sleep like Rip Van Winkle?
These sleepless nights don't help my bags,
That's why my face just sags and sags!

Time's a thief and surely will win
this fight with my crepe paper skin!

Popsicle Toes

Popsicle toes and a cherry nose,
I sneezed and shook and shivered;
Icicles hung from the rooftops,
Even birds froze as they quivered.

No matter how many socks I donned,
My toes turned purple and blue;
It got so bad I couldn't even put on a single shoe!

Every word I say is a frozen spray,
Little clouds of smoke from my lips;
Icicles form inside my nose as ol'
Jack Frost slyly nips.

Popsicle toes, I nearly froze
as I dragged my new red sled;
Down the hill, I took a spill,
I'd rather be warm in bed!

Those winter days of overcast haze
have now been left behind;
I took a ride down south for good,
Blue waters, where the sun always shined!

No boots for me, my toes are free
in sandals, flapping in the breeze;
No more popsicle toes and Rudolf's nose,
I'll have another Margarita, please!

My Last Diamond

(For my loving husband, Fred)

You're my last diamond ring on my hand,
The final vow, my last "I Do";
No ruby, emerald or sparkling gem
can ever replace my wonderful you!

You've got your own natural style,
the way you walk, that easy smile;
You found me when I was your diamond rough,
Times were hard, the going was tough.

But you loved me as if I was your treasure buried,
Like a pirate's dream, "First Mate", we married.

The smallest seed grows the mighty tree,
We stand tall together, you and me;
You're my last diamond, my love till the end,

As the saying goes,

"Diamonds Are A Girl's Best Friend"!

Printed in the United States
By Bookmasters